Sri Guru

LEARN TO SPEAK ENGLISH

Basic Sentences to Learn English

Youtube Channel: **Sri Guru Academy**

TITLE OF THE BOOK	:	**LEARN TO SPEAK ENGLISH**
AUTHOR	:	**Thanga Durai** M.A.,MPhil.,
FIRST EDITION	:	2019
SECOND EDITION	:	2026
PAGES	:	168
PRICE	:	200
ISBN NUMBER	:	978-81-998152-8-5
CONTACT NUMBER	:	7530008201
EMAIL ID	:	srigurupub@gmail.com
PUBLISHER (Imprint)	:	**Sri Guru Publication** Madurai.
PRINTER	:	Sri Meenakshi printers Madurai.

By the same Author:

Spoken English (English – Tamil)

Spoken English for Police and Advocate (Eng-Tam)

English In Business Field And It Sector

Speak English at School

Basic Question Answers for Communication

Basic Conversation

6000 Important Vocabulary for Life

1500 Children's Vocabulary

TIPS TO LEARN ENGLISH

- Surround yourself with English.
- Watch English Movies, Dramas, Documentaries, News channels etc.,
- Listen to English songs.
- Learn at least five new words per day.
- Often refer Dictionary.
- Read storybooks.
- Try to speak in English.
- Do not be afraid of making mistakes.
- Learn from Everyone.
- Learn some English Tongue Twister for better pronunciation.
- Try to write as much as you can.

S.No.	CONTENTS	Page No.

S.No.	CONTENTS	Page No.

1. TWO WORD SENTENCES

- Come in
- Come out
- Come fast
- Come first
- Come alone
- Come closer
- Come anytime
- Come here
- Come there
- Come near
- Come again
- Come inside
- Come afterwards
- Come forward
- Come tomorrow
- Go now
- Go inside
- Go out
- Go slow
- Go fast
- Go away
- Go up
- Go down
- Go home
- Go abroad
- Go faster

- Go tomorrow
- Go there
- Go again
- Get inside
- Please come
- Please move
- Please wait
- Please stop
- Please smile
- Please hurry
- Please read
- Excuse me
- Make way
- Get up
- Shut up
- Freshen up
- Get ready
- Get off
- Get away
- Get it
- Grow up
- Walk fast
- Walk slowly
- Warn him
- See you
- Stop here
- Stop crying
- Stop shouting

- Stop worrying
- Stop murmuring
- Stop joking
- Stop him
- Control yourself
- Check everyone
- Check again
- Wait outside
- Watch carefully
- Watch me
- Watch TV
- Well done!
- Wake up!
- Tell me
- Help me
- Save me
- Tell everybody
- Never forget
- Talk politely
- Taste this
- Take this
- Take it
- Take down
- Take rest
- Take care
- Take breakfast
- Take everything
- Try this

- Turn left
- Turn right
- Turn around
- Eat this
- Eat slowly
- Eat something
- Eat well
- Eat everything
- Everyone dreams
- Follow me
- Keep going
- Keep reading
- Keep this
- Use this
- Play well
- Play safe
- Look there
- Look here
- Let's go
- Let's see
- Do it
- Do business
- Do come
- Do nothing
- Try again
- Coming soon
- Choose one
- Choose carefully

- Cross it
- Record it
- Remind me
- Return immediately
- Save money
- Make money
- Pay cash
- Pay interest
- Save electricity
- Save time
- Save energy
- Sign here
- Stay there
- Sit here
- Seize him
- Catch him
- Study well
- Speak clearly
- Speak sensibly
- Speak up
- Someone came
- Keep driving
- Keep moving
- Never mind
- No problem
- How much?
- How many?
- How long?

- How soon?
- How far?
- How fast?
- How sad!
- How rude!
- How awful!
- How tragic!
- How come?
- How nice!
- How sweet!
- How peaceful!
- How soft!
- How old?
- How often?
- How big?
- How heavy?
- How deep?
- How tall?
- How high?
- Hold this.
- Why not?
- So what?
- What for?
- For what?
- To whom?
- From where?
- To where?
- Console him

- Fold them
- Put away
- Push back
- Hurry up!
- Be polite
- Be honest
- Be ready
- Be careful
- Behave yourself
- Enjoy yourself
- Me too
- Too much
- Too late
- Follow me
- I am
- I know
- Inform me
- Hold on
- Hold it
- Make sure
- Find yourself
- Say something
- Say please
- Say nothing
- Start singing
- Take action
- Take control
- Drive fast

- Drive slowly
- Drive carefully
- Nobody remembers
- Use this
- Leave it
- No way
- No chance
- No doubt
- Your turn
- Leave everything
- What nonsense!
- Who knows!
- Who cares!
- Nothing else
- Well done!
- My turn
- Just coming
- Smoke appeared
- They lost
- Think again
- Much better
- Have lunch
- Have patience
- Good news
- Bad news
- Good idea
- Good question
- My mistake

2. THREE WORD SENTENCES

- You did well.
- You got it.
- I am helpless.
- Are you crazy?
- Who is inside?
- Here he comes.
- Eat with us.
- He is rich.
- Who are you?
- I am Arun.
- Akash is sleeping.
- I feel shy.
- I feel sleepy.
- I feel feverish.
- Wake him up.
- Open the door.
- Close the door.
- Close your eyes.
- Come out now.
- Come and look.
- Come this way.
- Come get it.
- Clean the house.
- Cut the grass.
- Give me half.
- Give me those.

- Give a chair.
- Do your homework.
- Dreams come true.
- Deal with them.
- Take a break.
- Pay the bill.
- Put it down.
- Put it back.
- Write it down.
- Come on time.
- Come at once.
- Come down here.
- Come down slowly.
- Come see me.
- No one came.
- Wait and see.
- Call them in.
- Keep it up.
- Keep me advised.
- Keep me informed.
- Arrange a team.
- Break the rules.
- Break a record.
- Make an effort.
- Make a list.
- Tell my dad.
- Forget the past.
- Keep your promise.

- Keep the change.
- Put this on.
- Get a job.
- Back to work.
- Get the book.
- Keep it clean.
- Keep the keys.
- You work well.
- We live here.
- He tricked you.
- Somebody help me!
- Set him free.
- Set the table.
- Just roll up.
- Write me something.
- I believe you.
- I trust you.
- I respect you.
- I miss you.
- I want you.
- I saw nothing.
- Nobody saw me.
- It is good.
- It is bad.
- It is ok.
- Stay right here.
- Mind your business.
- Mind your step.

- Give me time.
- Give a speech.
- Reduce the volume.
- Stop playing inside.
- Lock the door.
- Come back soon.
- Come here soon.
- Bend your knees.
- Bear with me.
- Play with him.
- Remember the date.
- You work fast.
- Is it true?
- How is it?
- Your number, please.
- Your name, please.
- Please come in.
- Please sit down.
- Please sign here.
- Please help yourself.
- Please remember that.
- Please call me.
- Please do it.
- Please help me.
- Please tell me.
- Please fix that.
- Please be careful.
- I hate you.

- I hate this.
- Speak the truth.
- See the film.
- Just say no.
- Just keep walking.
- Just start walking.
- Stop irritating me.
- Everyone is ready.
- He tricked me.
- He came alone.
- Hold my hand.
- Hold it there.
- Hold the rope.
- I will continue.
- Deliver this message.
- My plan failed.
- Take a bath.
- Dry your hair.
- Wash your hair.
- Wash your face.
- Wipe your face.
- Comb your hair.
- Close the tap.
- Sweep the floor.
- Mop the floor.
- Remove your shirt.
- Wash the clothes.
- Change your clothes.

- Dry the clothes.
- Hang the clothes.
- Fold the mat.
- Open the window.
- Send me there.
- Make the bed.
- Make your bed.
- Purify the water.
- Heat the water.
- Water the plant.
- Mix the water.
- Sprinkle the water.
- Mow the lawn.
- Obey your elders.
- Have a heart.
- Clean the table.
- Clean your room.
- Consider my request.
- Keep it fun.
- Keep the money.
- Keep the change.
- Make it quick.
- Make it simple.
- Keep it simple.
- Let it be.
- Let it go.
- Let it pass.
- Let me pay.

- Let me practice.
- Let me explain.
- Tell me now.
- Tell me everything.
- Try to explain.
- Forgive my sins.
- Believe in yourself.
- Make your choice.
- Do your best.
- Do it now.
- Down your voice.
- Choose one person.
- Collect the money.
- Change is good.
- Make it happen.
- Learn from mistakes.
- Learn something new.
- Listen to me.
- Listen to this.
- It is possible.
- It's too much.
- Never give up.
- Love your job.
- Keep the faith.
- You are kidding.
- Do not lie.
- Stop playing around.
- Stop saying that.

- Come home early.
- Do come again.
- Call your mom.
- Cook at home.
- Get enough sleep.
- Wake up early.
- Get it yourself.
- Go to school.
- Get in line.
- Walk this way.
- Turn this way.
- Go to bed.
- Go to sleep.
- Make new friends.
- Take a walk.
- Go with her.
- Leave me alone.
- Bring the food.
- Who is coming?
- Come with me.
- Walk with me.
- Say it clearly.
- Come meet everybody.
- Try to understand.
- Try to remember.
- Take me home.
- Take me there.
- Take a rest.

- Turn on BBC.
- Turn that up.
- Never say that.
- Never be lazy.
- Now go away.
- Now go practice.
- No one understands.
- Winter has come.
- Come out quietly.
- Come on everybody.
- Cross the road.
- Go find out.
- Find somebody else.
- Go that way.
- Go over there.
- Make it real.
- Meet me there.
- Meet me downstairs.
- Play it again.
- Say it again.
- Everything's sold out.
- Send him in.
- Please shake hands.
- Shake my hand.
- Please sit here.
- Please explain it.
- Talk to me.
- Sing a song.

- Shut the door.
- Shut your mouth.
- Stop hitting me.
- Stand right there.
- Sing with us.
- Save your energy.
- Take a nap.
- Take my car.
- Take it easy.
- Tie your shoes.
- Throw them away.
- Throw the dice.
- Sit with me.
- Sit beside me.
- Step in closer.
- Speak with care.
- Find a job.
- Find the dog.
- Run and hide.
- Please find him.
- Return at once.
- Now turn around.
- Turn around slowly.
- One is missing.
- Nothing is missing.
- Loosen your tie.
- Turn it on.
- Turn it off.

- Light the candle.
- They heard crying.
- Everybody was sad.
- Ring the bell.
- The bell rang.
- Fix the watch.
- Stay and watch.
- Use my pen.
- Use your brain.
- Nobody visits Rohan.
- Hurry up, please.
- Leave it here.
- Leave me alone.
- Leave a message.
- Leave the building.
- Lead the way.
- Help the poor.
- Never forget that.
- She leads me.
- What a shame!
- What an idea!
- What a pity!
- What a sight!
- That is fantastic.
- Here we go.
- Here you go.
- Here you are.
- Hit the break.

- He grew old.
- Take this off.
- Wear warm clothes.
- He understands me.
- He underwent surgery.
- He just arrived.
- Ignore his request.
- He denied everything.
- Keep your promise.
- Keep them aside.
- Never give up.
- Never tell anyone.
- Twenty people attended.
- They arrived safely.
- Treat them well.
- He never lies.
- Never tell lies.
- Play it safe.
- Feed the dog.
- Rake the leaves.
- Paint the house.
- Please get up.
- I have lunch.
- Dry the dishes.
- Pack your lunch.
- Keep yourself clean.
- Go and play.
- Light the lamp.

- Button your shirt.
- Look at him.
- Look at me.
- Do the dishes.
- Do the laundry.
- Iron the clothes.
- Clean the windows.
- Clean the table.
- Do the washing.
- Come on everybody.
- Leave him alone.
- Train her well.
- Come with us.
- What a scene!
- Do forgive me!
- Feel at home.
- Not too far.
- Keep in touch.
- Signal is weak.
- Caught the ball.
- Start the camera.
- That’s not fair.
- Somebody help me!
- As you wish.
- Just like this.
- You did well.
- You trick me.
- Fold your bed-sheet.

- Sorry wrong number.
- Finish your breakfast.
- Listen to this.
- She is kind.
- I can lift.
- I can win.
- I can dance.
- I can run.
- I can jump.
- I can explain.
- I feel sleepy.
- I feel hungry.
- I feel giddy.
- I feel feverish.
- I feel nausea.
- I am happy.
- I am sick.
- I am lucky.
- I am busy.
- I am fit.
- I am nervous.
- I am sad.
- I am tired.
- I am sleepy.
- I am confused.
- I am angry.
- I am furious.
- I am unmarried.

- I am pregnant.
- I am poor.
- I am sorry.
- I am safe.
- I am clever.
- I am thirsty.
- I am here.
- I am improving.
- I am helpless.
- I am stuck.
- I go jogging.
- I know English.
- I already checked.
- I believe you.
- I lost it.

3. FOUR WORD SENTENCES

- I can do it.
- I can get it.
- I can see this.
- I can move this.
- I can fix it.
- I can stop it.
- I can come back.
- I can save you.
- I made a deal.
- I can make it.

- I can beat it.
- I have a bike.
- I have a dog.
- I have a balloon.
- The dog is digging.
- I have a pen.
- I hit the ball.
- The bat is here.
- I see the bus.
- I see a cat.
- I see my bike.
- I like my bike.
- I like my dog.
- I like to play.
- I see a boy.
- The boy is up.
- The girl is down.
- He fixes the car.
- The pot is hot.
- The pot is big.
- The flower is yellow.
- The book is red.
- I want a pen.
- I want to draw.
- Hide in the closet.
- Stick to your plan.
- He made a bet.
- He wins every time.

- I lost the bet.
- This is a key.
- This is a knife.
- This is a kite.
- This is a ball.
- This is a pen.
- The pen is blue.
- This is an apple.
- The apple is red.
- It is a pen.
- It is a watch.
- It is an apple.
- It is a box.
- Never tell a lie.
- Come on, wake up.
- That is very sad.
- Clean up this mess.
- Are your hands clean?
- This table is clean.
- Everything has been arranged.
- Give it to me.
- Give it to her.
- Give me a job.
- Give me your book.
- Give me a reason.
- Give me a chance.
- Give me the file.
- Gather your toys together.

- Lend me a hand.
- I am extremely sorry.
- I am the youngest.
- This is not true.
- I cannot help you.
- It's only a rumor.
- Explain that to me.
- How genius you are!
- Have a good day.
- Take care of yourself.
- Here is my hat.
- Here is my friend.
- I admit my mistake.
- Invite whomever you like.
- A ceasefire was declared.
- I accept the offer.
- I refused at first.
- Every member must attend.
- They arrived in time.
- I reached my goal.
- He never woke up.
- She never said no.
- Come into the room.
- Do it at once.
- Come home at once.
- Come along with me.
- Sounds good to me.
- Something must be done.

- Never try, never now.
- Do as you please!
- Do as we say!
- What's done is done.
- Here is the bill.
- Go away from here.
- Get off the bus.
- Get off the train.
- Describe what happened next.
- Hang up the laundry.
- Take out the rubbish.
- Please pack it up.
- Wait for an hour.
- Keep it and leave.
- I have a cold.
- I have a cough.
- I have a fever.
- I have an earache.
- I have a toothache.
- That is too much.
- That would be nice.
- Thanks for this honour.
- Return it to me.
- The situation is worrying.
- Go out with friends.
- Allow others to speak.
- Listen carefully to others.
- Of course, I am.

- As you say father.
- Laugh all you want.
- Call him at once.
- Let me show you.
- Listen to me carefully.
- Focus on the work.
- Please wake him up.
- Zip up your pants.
- Please get some water.
- Come and help me.
- Come and see me.
- Look after the baby.
- Be a good girl.
- Turn off the TV.
- Turn on the light.
- Switch off the phone.
- Send me a message.
- My battery is down.
- Our duty is over.
- Out of the way.
- Look, there goes Kevin.
- Look! There he comes.
- Here comes the principal!
- Take me to him.
- Do tell us, please!
- Give them to me.
- Have pity on me!

4. SIMPLE QUESTION AND ANSWERS

- What is your name?
  My name is Arun.
- What is your father's name?
  My father's name is Anand.
- What are you doing?
  I am studying.
- What is your father?
  He is a Teacher.
- What is your mother?
  She is a homemaker.
- What is your sister?
  She is studying in college.
- What is your age?
  My age is 16.
- What is your hobby?
  My hobby is reading.
- Who is he?
  He is my friend.
- Who is she?
  She is my sister.
- Who are they?
  They are my friends.
- Who are you?
  I am a student.
- Who beat you?
  Arun beats me.

- Who is this?
  This is my friend.
- Who is your friend?
  Arun is my friend.
- Who is driving?
  Anand is driving.
- Where are you from?
  I am from Delhi.
- Where is my book?
  It is on the table.
- Where are you?
  I am in home.
- How old are you?
  I am 23 years old.
- How old is she?
  She is 18.
- What time is it?
  It is 10 o'clock.
- What is she doing?
  She is cooking.
- When do you wake up?
  I wake up at 6 a.m.
- When is your birthday?
  My birthday is on 26th January.
- When will you come?
  I will come tomorrow.
- When will you go?
  I will go tonight.

- Whose phone is this?
  It is mine.
- Why are you late?
  The bus was late.
- Do you go to school?
  Yes, I go to school.
- Do you live here?
  Yes, I live here.
- Do you smoke?
  No, I don't smoke.
- Do you like it?
  Yes, I like it.
- Did you sleep well?
  Yes, I slept well.
- Did you close the door?
  Yes, I closed the door.
- Did you eat lunch?
  No, I didn't eat lunch.
- Did you go to school?
  Yes, I went to school.
- May I come in?
  Yes, come in.
- Are you happy?
  Yes, I am happy.
- Are you ready?
  I am ready.
- Are you hungry?
  Yes, I am hungry.

- Are you married?
  Yes, I am married.
- Are you lazy?
  No, I am not lazy.
- Are you busy?
  Yes, I am busy.
- Can you speak English?
  Yes, I can speak English.
- What are you doing?
  I am writing.
- What is he doing?
  He is studying.
- What is she doing?
  She is sleeping.
- What did you eat?
  I ate noodles.
- What do you have lunch?
  I have veg-biriyani.
- Is it good?
  Yes, it is good.
- Is it true?
  No, it is not true.
- Is it yours?
  Yes, it is mine.
- Is he Vimal?
  Yes, he is Vimal.
- Is she the manager?
  Yes, she is the manager.

- Is he eating?
  Yes, he is eating.
  No, he is not eating.
- Is she playing?
  Yes, she is playing.
  No, she is not playing.
- Are you writing?
  Yes, I am writing.
  No, I am not writing.
- Are they sleeping?
  Yes, they are sleeping.
  No, they are not sleeping.

5. HOBBIES

- I watch TV.
- I listen to music.
- I read a book.
- I write stories.
- I read the newspaper.
- I paint.
- I draw.
- I take selfie.
- I take photos.
- I spend time with my family.
- I sing.
- I dance.
- I surf the internet.

- I read magazines.
- I chat with my friends.
- I play with my toys.
- I play cards.
- I watch videos online.
- I read news online.
- I take a nap.
- I fly a kite.
- I play on a swing.
- I go to the gym.
- I go to the park.
- I go to the library.
- I go shopping.
- I go to the movies.
- I go for a walk.
- I play sports.
- I play chess.
- I play with friends.
- I play the drums.
- I do crosswords.
- I do the gardening.
- I do yoga.
- I ride my bike.
- I learn new languages.
- I look at the stars.
- I get my nails done.
- I knit.
- I blow bubbles.

- I plant trees.
- I play Frisbee.
- I play with my dog.
- I check my social media accounts.

6. DAILY CHORES

- I wake up early.
- I get up.
- I brush my teeth.
- I wash my face.
- I take a shower.
- I take bath.
- I dry my hair.
- I get dressed.
- I comb my hair.
- I make breakfast.
- I eat breakfast.
- I go to school.
- I take classes.
- I go to work.
- I start work at 10.
- I have lunch.
- I finish school.
- I finish work at five.
- I come home at 6 p.m.
- I arrive home.
- I do my homework.

- I go to tuition.
- I cook dinner.
- I eat dinner.
- I watch TV.
- I go to bed.
- I fall asleep.

7. OCCUPATION

- I am a student.
- I am a graduate.
- I am unemployed.
- She is a doctor.
- She is a nurse.
- She is an accountant.
- She is a beautician.
- She is a cook.
- She is a pilot.
- She is a tailor.
- She is a chef.
- She is a principal.
- She is a manager.
- She is a maid.
- She is a washerwoman.
- She is a florist.
- He is a teacher.
- He is a lecturer.
- He is an engineer.

- He is a mechanic.
- He is a plumber.
- He is an astrologer.
- He is an auditor.
- He is a broker.
- He is a barber.
- He is a grocer.
- He is a driver.
- He is an advocate.
- He is a baker.
- He is a washer man.
- He is a surveyor.
- He is a police.
- He is a scientist.
- He is a headmaster.
- He is a physical trainer.
- He is a body builder.
- He is a supervisor.
- He is a draper.
- You are a prohit.
- You are a merchant.
- You are a publisher.
- You are a postman.
- You are a police officer.
- You are a bookseller.
- You are a security guard.
- You are a patient.
- You are an athlete.

- You are a carpenter.
- You are a servant.
- We are soldiers.
- We are dentists.
- We are students.
- We are teachers.
- We are doctors.
- We are officers.
- They are trainers.
- They are athletes.
- They are actors.
- They are traders.
- My mother is a homemaker.
- My father is a businessman.
- My brother is an engineer.
- My sister is a teacher.
- My uncle is a doctor.

8. PRESENT CONTINUOUS TENSE

What are you doing?

- I am writing.
- I am studying.
- I am reading.
- I am listening.
- I am crying.
- I am fighting.
- I am watching.

- I am eating.
- I am playing.
- I am sleeping.
- I am searching.
- I am working.
- I am going.
- I am coming.
- I am thinking.
- I am waiting.
- I am seeing.
- I am running.
- I am walking.
- I am feeling.
- I am returning.
- I am binding.
- I am telling.
- I am driving.
- I am hearing.
- I am holding.
- I am singing.
- I am visiting.
- I am worrying.
- I am leaving.
- I am drinking.
- I am taking.
- I am cooking.
- I am looking.
- I am cleaning.

- I am buying.
- I am dreaming.
- I am selling.
- I am riding.
- I am weeping.
- I am collecting.
- I am explaining.
- I am describing.
- I am inviting.
- I am attending.

What is he doing?

- He is writing.
- He is studying.
- He is reading book.
- He is listening.
- He is crying.
- He is fighting.
- He is watching.
- He is eating.
- He is playing.
- He is sleeping.
- He is searching.
- He is working.
- He is going.
- He is coming.
- He is thinking.
- He is waiting.

- He is seeing.
- He is running.
- He is walking.
- He is feeling.
- He is returning.
- He is binding.
- He is telling.
- He is driving.
- He is hearing.
- He is holding.
- He is singing.
- He is visiting.
- He is worrying.
- He is leaving.
- He is drinking.
- He is taking.
- He is cooking.
- He is looking.
- He is cleaning.
- He is buying.
- He is dreaming.
- He is selling.
- He is riding.
- He is weeping.
- He is collecting.
- He is explaining.
- He is describing.
- He is inviting.

- He is attending.

What is she doing?

- She is writing.
- She is studying.
- She is reading.
- She is listening.
- She is crying.
- She is fighting.
- She is watching TV.
- She is eating.
- She is playing chess.
- She is sleeping.
- She is searching.
- She is working.
- She is going.
- She is coming.
- She is thinking.
- She is waiting.
- She is seeing.
- She is running.
- She is walking.
- She is feeling.
- She is returning.
- She is binding.
- She is telling.
- She is driving.
- She is hearing.

- She is holding.
- She is singing.
- She is visiting.
- She is worrying.
- She is leaving.
- She is drinking.
- She is taking.
- She is cooking.
- She is looking.
- She is cleaning.
- She is buying.
- She is dreaming.
- She is selling.
- She is riding.
- She is weeping.
- She is collecting.
- She is explaining.
- She is describing.
- She is inviting.
- She is attending.

What are they doing?

- They are writing homework.
- They are studying English.
- They are reading newspaper.
- They are listening music.
- They are crying.
- They are fighting.

- They are watching TV.
- They are eating biriyani.
- They are playing football.
- They are sleeping in the room.
- They are searching everywhere.
- They are working in a private company.
- They are going to temple.
- They are coming from Delhi.
- They are thinking.
- They are waiting for you.
- They are seeing.
- They are running.
- They are walking on the bridge.
- They are feeling.
- They are returning from Chennai.
- They are binding the book.
- They are telling the truth.
- They are hearing songs.
- They are holding.
- They are singing a song.
- They are visiting.
- They are worrying about the incident.
- They are leaving airport.
- They are drinking coffee.
- They are taking rest.
- They are cooking.
- They are looking at me.
- They are cleaning the house.

- They are buying vegetables.
- They are selling clothes.
- They are riding.
- They are collecting the money.
- They are explaining the incident.
- They are describing.
- They are inviting the guests.
- They are attending the meeting.

You are….

- You are writing.
- You are studying.
- You are reading.
- You are listening.
- You are crying.
- You are fighting.
- You are watching.
- You are eating.
- You are playing.
- You are sleeping.
- You are searching.
- You are working.
- You are going.
- You are coming.
- You are thinking.
- You are waiting.
- You are seeing.
- You are running.

- You are walking.
- You are feeling.
- You are returning.
- You are binding.
- You are telling.
- You are driving.
- You are hearing.
- You are singing.
- You are worrying.
- You are leaving.
- You are drinking.
- You are taking.
- You are cooking.
- You are looking.
- You are cleaning.
- You are buying.
- You are dreaming.
- You are selling.
- You are riding.
- You are weeping.
- You are collecting.
- You are describing.
- You are inviting.

We are….

- We are writing.
- We are studying.
- We are reading.

- We are listening.
- We are crying.
- We are fighting.
- We are watching.
- We are eating.
- We are playing.
- We are sleeping.
- We are searching.
- We are working.
- We are going.
- We are coming.
- We are thinking.
- We are waiting.
- We are running.
- We are walking.
- We are feeling.
- We are returning.
- We are binding.
- We are telling.
- We are driving.
- We are hearing.
- We are holding.
- We are singing.
- We are visiting.
- We are leaving.
- We are drinking.
- We are taking.
- We are cooking.

- We are cleaning.
- We are buying.
- We are selling.
- We are collecting.
- We are explaining.
- We are describing.
- We are inviting.

9. 'Don't Sentences

- Don't go
- Don't come
- Don't wait
- Don't cry
- Don't move
- Don't cheat
- Don't shout
- Don't save
- Don't talk
- Don't play
- Don't ask
- Don't sit
- Don't run
- Don't open
- Don't close
- Don't eat
- Don't jump
- Don't sleep

- Don't tell
- Don't sing
- Don't laugh
- Don't drive
- Don't worry
- Don't drink
- Don't break
- Don't take
- Don't touch
- Don't cook
- Don't buy
- Don't cut
- Don't dig
- Don't fight
- Don't forget
- Don't hide
- Don't send
- Don't turn
- Don't call
- Don't walk
- Don't give
- Don't stand
- Don't tease
- Don't stop
- Don't change
- Don't teach
- Don't hurry
- Don't wash

- Don’t use
- Don’t read
- Don’t fold
- Don’t pinch

10. ‘Me’ Sentences

- Tell me
- Help me
- Give me
- Follow me
- Trust me
- Bless me
- Forgive me
- Save me
- Promise me
- Hold me
- Excuse me
- Leave me
- Send me
- Show me
- Hit me
- Find me
- Call me
- Push me
- Pull me
- Ask me
- Get me

- Advise me
- Use me
- Teach me
- Obey me
- Believe me
- Lead me
- Encourage me
- Marry me

11. GREETINGS

How are you?

- How are you?
- How is your mother?
- How is your dad?
- How is your wife?
- How is your family?
- How is your studies going?
- How about you?

Response to '**How are you?**'

- Fine.
- I am fine.
- I am good.
- She is fine.
- They are fine.
- It is going well.
- Not bad.

WELCOME

- You are welcome.
- Welcome home.
- Welcome to our home.
- Welcome to Madurai.
- I am so happy you could visit.
- You are welcome to join us.
- We received a warm welcome.
- You are always welcome here.

THANK YOU

- Thank you so much.
- Thanks for your help.
- Thanks for your advice.
- Thanks for the gift.
- Thank you for inviting me.
- Thank you for coming.

Response to '**thank you**'

- It is my pleasure.
- No problem.
- I am glad to help you.
- I am happy to be here.
- I am here to help
- It was nothing
- Don't mention it

CONGRATULATION

- Congratulation!
- Happy journey.
- Excellent!
- All the best.
- Nice job.
- You are doing well.
- Best wishes for you.

GOODBYE

- Goodbye!
- Take care.
- Keep in touch.
- Bye Bye! See you.
- See you again.
- See you soon.
- See you today evening.
- Convey my regards to your parents.

GLAD TO MEET YOU

- Nice to meet you
- Happy to meet you
- Nice to see you again
- It is a pleasure to meet you

12. INTRODUCE YOUR FRIEND

- Anbu, this is Rohan.
- This is Ram. He is studying with me.

- This is my friend Somu.
- That is Shreya.
- Mohan, let me introduce you to Arun.

YOU SEEM FAMILIAR

- I know you from somewhere.
- Have we met before?
- I am sure I have seen you before.
- I think we have met before.

13. PLACE

- Where do you live?
- Where is your home?
- Where are you from?
- Where do you stay?
- Where do you come from?
- Which is your native place?
- I live here.
- I live in Mumbai.
- I am from Bangalore.
- My native place is Chennai.
- I come from Kerala.
- He lives at Nethaji Street.
- I live at 25th Nehru Street.
- Is he residing here?
- He lives nearby.
- She lives in Chennai.
- He is my neighbour

14. DESCRIBING FAMILY

- Do you have any brothers or sisters?
- How large is your family?
- My family has five people my parents, my brother, sister and I.
- I am an only child.
- There are five members in our family.
- I have two brothers and a sister.
- I have two sisters.
- I have two brothers, one older and one younger.
- I have an elder brother and a younger sister.
- She is my elder sister.
- I don’t have any brothers and sisters.
- This is my cousin, Ananya.
- He is my younger brother.
- She is my grandmother.
- He is my grandfather.
- She is my mother-in-law.
- She is my paternal aunt.
- My uncle has a son and a daughter.
- He is my maternal uncle.
- Anand is my brother-in-law.
- Shreya is my sister-in-law.
- Suresh is my nephew.
- Meera is my niece.
- Ours is a joint family.
- Ours is a nuclear family.
- Ours is an orthodox family.

- Ours is a small family.
- I am from a big family.
- She comes from a big family.

15. AT HOME

- Please get up.
- Please wake him up.
- I do exercise in the morning.
- I brush my teeth.
- I brush my teeth twice a day.
- I take bath in the morning.
- I brush my hair every day.
- Keep yourself clean.
- I usually put on makeup.
- My alarm clock rang.
- I wake up at 6:00 am.
- I have a shower at 7:00 am.
- I drink milk in the morning.
- I eat breakfast at 7:30 am.
- I take breakfast at 9 o'clock.
- I have breakfast at eight-thirty.
- I take the bus at nine o'clock.
- I eat lunch at 12:30 pm.
- I eat dinner at 7:00 pm.
- I get home at 4:00 pm.
- I go to bed at 9:00 pm.
- I do my chores.
- I wake up.

- I brush my teeth.
- I wash my face.
- I go to bathroom.
- I take a shower.
- I dry my hair.
- I get dressed.
- I comb my hair in the morning.
- My hair has grown too long.
- I eat breakfast.
- I go to school.
- I study.
- I have lunch.
- I come home.
- I do my homework.
- I watch TV in the evening.
- I have dinner.
- I go to sleep.
- I sleep at ten o'clock.
- Sometimes I skip breakfast.
- Please wake me up at five tomorrow morning.
- There is no towel in the bathroom.
- Can I have a towel, please?
- I haven't finished drying my hair yet.
- She will do the dishes.
- Do the dishes.
- Dry the dishes.
- Put the utensils in the drawer.
- Vimala is sweeping the floor.

- I clean up my room every Sunday.
- Scrub the floor with a brush.
- My clothes are filthy.
- Your shirt is dirty.
- Put dirty clothes in the basket.
- Take off your shirt.
- My mother is washing the clothes.
- Wring the clothes.
- I do the laundry.
- I do laundry in the morning.
- This stain is not washing out.
- Do not bleach.
- Wash in cold water.
- Please wash these clothes.
- Hang the clothes to dry.
- The clothesline is full.
- Hang your shirts up.
- Is my laundry ready?
- Do you do the ironing?
- Don't iron.
- Don't fold them.
- Button up your shirt.
- Zip up your pants.
- He needs new shoes.
- The chocolate is for you.
- Where is the mixi?
- The mixi is in the corner.
- My lunchtime is at noon.

- I eat dinner in the evening.
- I watch TV in the evening.
- Put the things in order.
- Put the comb in its place.
- Do you do any cooking yourself?
- Don’t eat fast.
- Don’t gulp your food.
- Dust the furniture.
- Vacuum the carpet.
- Set the table.
- Clear the table.
- Could you please wipe the table?
- Clean the sink.
- Can I help you clean up?
- Clean up after eating.
- There are many cobwebs in the corner.
- Clean the cobweb.
- Your room is spick and span.
- Dispose the rubbish.
- Tidy up your room.
- Don’t make a mess in the house.
- If you make a mess, clean it up.
- Do housework.
- Take out the garbage.
- Bring me a bucket of water.
- Sprinkle the water.
- Turn on the sprinklers.
- Come and help me.

- Mop the floor.
- Clean the floor with water.
- Pour the water on the floor and clean it.
- My mother often cleans the house.
- Pour the water in utensil.
- My mom does house work at six o’clock.
- You should make your bed.
- Don’t jump on the bed.
- Don’t dump everything on the bed.
- Stay out of my room.
- Don’t stay up late every night.
- Dad is going to scold you when he sees this!
- I need a new bedspread.
- Replace the old blankets.
- Change the pillow cover.
- Here’s a pillow you can use.
- Fold your bed-sheet.
- Where is your mother?
- My mother is cooking.
- She has gone to market.
- My mother is not at home.
- She has gone out.
- She buys vegetable in the market.
- She is sleeping.
- She is at home.
- She stays at home and looks after the children.
- He is just a kid.
- The baby is crying.

- Look after the baby.
- You take care now.
- The baby fell asleep in the cradle.
- Look after your sister.
- Don't let him touch it.
- Don't leave her alone.
- Don't go anywhere without me.
- I should be with my family.
- I stayed at home last night.
- We usually visit our grandparents a couple of times a month.
- Take the chair.
- Put the chair back in place.
- My father fixed a broken chair.
- I got my ears pierced.
- My mother cooks at eleven o'clock.
- My mom has lunch at one o'clock.
- At what time is sunrise?
- At what time is sunset?
- Do you go to college?
- When will breakfast be ready?
- At what time do you usually go to school?
- I usually go to school at 8am.
- I am preparing my kids.
- Have you attended the school today?
- Have you gone to school today?
- I attended the school today.
- I went to school today.
- I couldn't go to school today, I was sick.

- I read the newspaper every day.
- I frequently speak with my friends on the phone.
- Put the things in the box.
- I said put it down!
- Take it or leave it.
- Put the jewel in the casket.
- I will take this one instead of that one.
- I miss the home-cooked meal.
- Let's hang this photo on the wall.
- What are you looking for?
- I am looking for the specs.
- I cannot find it anywhere.
- Are you ready to go to school?
- Get ready for school.
- Get dressed and ready for school.
- It is time for school.
- Keep everything ready.
- Pack my lunch.
- She packs her school bag.
- Where is my pant?
- Tuck your shirt in.
- Put on the shoes.
- Where are my socks?
- Where are my shoes?
- Those are my shoes.
- I cannot find my pen.
- Fill up the ink in the pen.
- Where is the inkpot?

- Never miss the prayer.
- Take off your shoes.
- How stinky your socks are!
- My passport is nowhere to be found.
- Where is my phone?
- It is on the table.
- It is in the drawer.
- It is behind the TV.
- It is near the box.
- It is above the table.
- It is to the left of the table.
- It is between the boxes.
- It is next to the desk.
- It is in front of the TV.
- It is under the table.
- It is over the door.
- It is opposite to the box.
- See for yourself.
- Switch on the fan.
- Switch off the fan.
- Put the fan on high speed.
- Put the thing in the cupboard.
- I cannot close the door.
- The door is stuck.
- I make dinner.
- We cook food on the stove.
- The food is ready.
- Come on everybody. It's time to eat.

- Wash your hands.
- What is for dinner tonight?
- Is dinner ready?
- You cook the same dishes all the time.
- Put the waste food away.
- Don’t spill the milk.
- If you spill it, clean it up.
- Let’s go downstairs.
- Are you at home?
- He came home at eight.
- Do not sit idle.
- You don’t do anything.
- Don’t go back to sleep.
- You rest all day.
- Go and play with your friends.
- Get me the newspaper.
- Pick up the toys.
- Don't rub the floor.
- You may fall down.
- Her room is always out of order.
- Did you lock the door?
- If you open it, close it.
- Please get some water.
- May I have a glass of water?
- Fetch me a glass of water.
- Put the flour in utensil.
- Go and take some rest.
- Answer the phone call.

- Drink your milk.
- This tea is very hot.
- My sister lives apart.
- Light the lamp.
- If you turn it on, turn it off.
- Turn off the light.
- Turn on the lights.
- I turned the lamp off.
- It's dark in here. Turn on the lights.
- Did you turn off the gas?
- I am shivering.
- It is very cold.
- Heat the water.
- Can you please turn on the heating?
- Can you please turn off the heating?
- Shall we go to supermarket?
- Where are you going?
- I am going to the shop.
- Shall we go for a walk?
- Who is he?
- He is my elder brother.
- This is my younger brother.
- He is my grandfather.
- He is my neighbour.
- He is my classmate.
- He is my colleague.
- Who is she?
- She is my mother.

- She is my elder sister.
- She is my younger sister.
- She is my grandmother.
- Vimala! Is that you? What a big girl?
- How time flies?
- She has grown up.
- Be a good girl.
- I wonder who that girl is.
- She resembles her mother.
- She got her mother's nose.
- He looks just like his father.
- You are a lot like your father.
- How old are you?
- You are a good boy.
- He is incorrigible.
- Whom to vote?
- Who is coming to the marriage?
- Which would you like meat or fish?
- I will take a nap after lunch.
- I lost my ring.
- I got my haircut.
- He lives on his pension.
- What colour is your house?
- Someone sent you this courier.
- I had a good dream last night.
- He invited me to his house.
- Nancy invited him to her birthday party.
- I am happy and excited.

- The house is beautiful.
- Everyone in my family is rich.
- He is not able to buy a car.
- The washing machine doesn't work.
- It stopped working yesterday.
- Have you called the repairman?
- If you don't know how to operate, leave it.
- If you can't fix the problem, call in someone who can.
- I am running late.
- What time is it?
- I have a dog and his name is puppy.
- My dog is only three months old.
- Don't let the dog out.
- My dog has gone missing.
- Don't keep the door open.
- Don't get close to the fire.
- Don't leave the lights on.
- Who left the tap running?
- You are grown men. Act like it.
- Can you stay and watch the children?
- You are such a beautiful baby.
- Don't worry. Your son will be well taken care of.
- Don't talk to the strangers.
- Keep an eye on the kids.
- Please be home by five o'clock.
- Whenever possible, you come here.
- My father took us to the park.
- Don't go yet.

- Do as I say.
- Don't scold like that.
- I like fish better than meat.
- Here is your coffee.
- Watch out, it's hot.
- I drink coffee without sugar.
- I have to eat hereafter.
- Behave yourself.
- Act like a lady.
- Act like a gentleman.
- My parents died when I was six.
- Your problem and mine are similar.
- Stop it.
- Don't touch that.
- How many times have I told you?
- Don't make me tell you again.
- Put that down.
- Stop teasing your brother.
- Don't be naughty.
- Why are you crying?
- Don't play.
- Leave him alone.
- Go to bed on time.
- My children are already asleep.
- I will leave my house at 9:00.
- What happened?
- I fell off the bike.
- I met with an accident.

- Why are you limping?
- My foot hurts.
- I hurt my back.
- I will be home late today.
- Don't wait for me.
- Don't wake me up.
- Are you going to wear that dress to the function?
- Did you buy what I asked you to buy?
- Would you like something to drink?
- What would you like to drink?
- I usually don't drink coffee.
- Feel at home.
- Make yourself at home.
- What about others?
- Everyone is in the living room.
- She is in the kitchen.
- It is almost time for dinner.
- Can you stay and have dinner with us?
- Shall I accompany you?
- Why don't you stay here?
- Please come again.
- Let's eat out tonight.
- We are not very hungry yet.
- I am so happy to be home.
- Come and visit us again.
- What are you watching?
- I left my umbrella in the bus.
- Did you go to church last Sunday?

- What is on television tonight?
- Please move the TV set to the right.
- What channel is this?
- Let’s change the channel.
- Please turn up the TV volume.
- Reduce the volume.
- Don’t sit so close to the television.
- Hand me the remote control.
- Turn on the TV.
- Turn off the TV.
- Turn up the volume.
- Turn down the volume.
- That TV doesn’t work.
- I spent all day by watching TV.
- I saw that movie on TV last month.
- Let’s stay home and watch TV tonight.
- She doesn’t listen to me.
- Where is the carpet?
- Clean your shoes on the mat.
- There is so much mud on the carpet.
- I do not know. It is not mine.
- I don’t wear a watch.
- They look clean.
- It is covered with dust.
- Mummy, could I have some snacks please?
- I am hungry.
- Make him eat.
- Do you have anything to eat?

- There is nothing in the fridge.
- I didn't see it.
- Oh, here it is.
- I don't buy it.
- I don't own a car.
- That car is hers.
- Thanks for driving me home.
- I listen to the radio.
- Your room smells bad.
- Do you smell that?
- It smells normal to me.
- It smells like there is rotten food somewhere.
- Whose room is that?
- This is my son's room.
- What room is that?
- That is the bathroom.
- Where is Ram?
- He is in his room.
- Are they bed bug bites?
- I did not sleep well.
- I have a dream last night.
- Where will you pick me?
- When will you be back?
- Mom, I am going to my friend's house.
- Arun, what are you saying?
- Mom please, may I go out to play?
- You won't go outside until you finish your homework.
- I am really sorry for yelling at you.

- I don't argue with my mom and dad.
- I found a 500 rupee note on the street today.
- Are you going out?
- Is Reena at home?
- I want to see her.
- She is not at home now.
- Aakash is out with his friends.
- Shall I come back later?
- I am having trouble with my bike.
- Keep all the doors locked.
- Turn the knob and open the door.
- There is someone at the door.
- Someone came to see you.
- Who's there?
- No one is there.
- I don't know.
- Mom, someone is here to meet you.
- Do you have a place to stay?
- How long have you been living here?
- I have been living here for the past ten years.
- Do you live around here?
- I live next door.
- I have never seen you before.
- I don't have any friends here.
- Could I use your bathroom, please?
- He and I share a room.
- May I know your name?
- There are four members in our family.

- She bore him three children.
- Malar has given birth to a baby boy.
- Are you looking for Dr. Praveen?
- Do you know where he lives?
- They have moved to their new house.
- I know almost everyone here.
- I grew up here.
- Is your wife home?
- When are you moving to the new house?
- Do you know who it is?
- I am the owner of this building.
- I know his family.
- There is no water problem at all.
- I can't pay my rent.
- I am in a lot of trouble.
- I won't stay any longer.
- My house is beautiful.
- This house needs painting.
- My house is painted white.
- My house is spacious enough for me.
- Every room in my house has two windows.
- Do you live alone?
- Where do you stay?
- Where is your home?
- Where do you come from?
- Do you live here?
- I live here since1970.
- I live here for 30 years

- Bharat lives in a flat.
- She lives in an Apartment.
- I live in a two-bedroom apartment.
- I live on the fifth floor.
- He lives alone.
- I don't like living here.
- I don't know those people.
- You will die if you stay here.
- Our house is near the city centre.
- My house is five blocks away.
- I sold my house last month.
- I didn't plan to go anywhere.
- They got married quickly.
- My husband left me.
- He married my sister.
- He is married to Radha.
- Do you two already know each other?
- Put on your night suit.
- My daughter sleeps in the cot next to my bed.
- I kept tossing and turning all night.
- I cannot sleep all the night.
- It is time to sleep.
- I am going to sleep.

16. DESCRIBING PEOPLE

- What does she look like?
- How tall she is?
- He is only 6 feet.

- He is strong.
- Ramesh is tall.
- He is lanky.
- He is quite short.
- He is a dwarf.
- He is not very tall.
- She is fat.
- Ananya is of medium height.
- She is lean.
- Anitha is slim.
- She has blue/brown eyes.
- He has big/small eyes.
- Nancy has big round eyes.
- Her eyes are blue colour.
- She has thin lips.
- Nancy has curved lips.
- She has full lips.
- What colour is his/her hair?
- Is her hair long or short?
- I have got a ponytail.
- She has long black hair.
- She has shoulder-length hair.
- Emily has long hair.
- Latha has short hair.
- She has medium length blonde hair.
- His hair is black.
- I have got curly hair.
- He has got straight hair.

- My friend has a white beard.
- My hair is wavy.
- His hair is spiky.
- She is blonde.
- Her hair is short.
- Samantha has curly hair.
- She has lovely hair.
- She has big eyes and long hair.
- He has dark eyes and black hair.
- I have an oval face.
- She has a round face.
- She has a triangle face.
- He has a long face.
- Matilda has a round face.
- He has small/long nose.
- She has straight nose.
- She has turned-up nose.
- Maria has got flat nose.
- She has got pointed nose.
- She has large mouth.
- He has small mouth.
- What is his body type?
- She is a chubby kid.
- You are a little husky.
- She is a little plump (fleshy).
- This girl is petite (short).
- She is too skinny (lean).
- She is overweight.

- Tell me how he looks like.
- He is manly/muscular.
- He is hairy.
- He is dark.
- He is classy.
- My sister is so beautiful.
- Sam is a thick-skinned person.
- He is a laid-back.
- He has beard/goatee.
- He has moustache.
- They are well-dressed.
- He is unfashionable.
- He wears specs.
- He has a killer smile.
- He has six packs.
- The boy is naughty.
- He is rude.
- Sam, you look very nice today.
- She is upset.
- Manoj is an anxious person.
- My mom is very affectionate.
- My Dad is bad-tempered.
- My father is very strict.
- My mother is friendly.
- He is aggressive.
- He is a bit boring.
- She is very creative.
- You look very cute.

- You look gorgeous!
- She is pretty.
- He is good-looking.
- How handsome you are!
- He is smart.
- She is attractive.
- Vani is very helpful.
- She is a good friend of mine.
- Vimala is an athletic.
- She is a very attractive woman.
- You look like a celebrity.
- You are still very young.
- You look drop dead gorgeous!
- Wow, you are gorgeous!
- You look great today.
- You are so adorable!
- You look so radiant!
- You look fabulous in this dress.
- He is stunning.
- She is ugly.
- Kamal was tall, dark, and handsome.
- You look lovely tonight.
- She is not so charming.
- You look stunning in that dress.
- You look beautiful!
- You are so cute!
- Jyothika is not so beautiful.
- Malar is blue eyed, tall and lean.

- You look fantastic!
- Anitha has such a cute daughter.
- He is handsome.
- He is a funny person.
- She is arrogant.
- Ajay is very courageous.
- Sneha is very dependable.
- He is very sociable.
- Leela is introverted.
- He is industrious.
- My sister is very naughty.
- My brother is innocent.
- Rohan is stupid.
- She is lazy.
- He is very active.
- He is a joker.
- He is head turner.
- He is a flirt.
- He is a womanizer.
- He is a dumb.
- Rahul is ambitious.
- They are witty.
- I am mad.
- He is crazy.
- He is a liar.
- He is a mother's boy.
- He is a bad boy.
- He is a charming.

- Danush is romantic.
- He is rich.
- He is a good dresser.
- He makes me laugh.
- Ajit has killer eyes.
- She looks pale.
- You look worried.
- She is optimistic.
- He is a pessimist.
- He is very thoughtful.
- He is a gentleman.
- Thomas is a hard working person.
- She is an artistic woman.
- He is a charismatic politician.
- She is sad.
- He is very joyful.
- Kamal is a sympathetic person.
- He is a talkative person.
- She is a chatterbox.
- He is a hen-pecked man.
- I am really out going.
- Rohit is a social butterfly.
- Arun is very friendly.
- I am a gregarious person.
- I am a kind of reserved.
- He is a good listener.
- Krish is a selfish fellow.
- He looks good.

17. TALKING ABOUT AGE

- How old are you?
- How old is she?
- How old are they?
- How old is your father?
- What is your age?
- I am 30 years old.
- She is 16 years.
- I was born in 1980.
- They are 45 years old.
- I graduated at 25.
- I got married at 28.
- Next month, I am turning 26.
- His parents died when he was six.
- John is 18 and Arun is 21.
- I am 12 and my brother is 16.
- Rohan will be turning 8 years next year.
- She turned 18 years old last year.
- He is my age.
- She was about eight years old.

18. WAIT

- Wait for me.
- Please wait a minute.
- I don't have time to wait.
- Just wait and see.
- Please wait until I come back.

- Please wait here.
- Wait here until I return.
- Just wait here.
- Don't go, wait for me.
- kamal is waiting.
- The car is waiting for you.
- I am waiting near a bus stop.
- Please wait, I will come.
- I will wait for you.
- Come on! I can't wait any more.
- Don't wait for me.

19. READY

- Are you ready?
- I am ready.
- Are they ready?
- Yes, they are ready.
- Are you ready to go to theatre?
- Yes, I am ready to go.
- Is lunch ready?
- Yes, it is ready.
- No, it is not ready.
- The food is ready.
- I am not ready.

20. HURRY

- Hurry up!

- Please hurry.
- I am in hurry now.
- Why are you in hurry?
- Why such a hurry?
- Hurry up! You will miss your bus.
- Let's go, it is time.
- Come on, It is too late.

21. KITCHEN

- Switch on the stove.
- Take the pan.
- Keep it on the stove.
- Heat the pan.
- Heat the oil.
- Fry the onion.
- Take bowl.
- Mix well.
- Stir well.
- Beat well.
- Add salt.
- Mix it together.
- Peel the onion.
- Chop the onion.
- Chop the vegetables.
- Whisk the egg white.
- Spread the butter.
- Melt the butter.
- Bake the cake.

- Beat the egg.
- Add little salt.
- Add little water.
- Pour some water.
- Knead the dough.
- Knead it well.
- Make a big roll.
- Make a ball.
- Flatten the dough.
- Grease your hands with oil.
- Knead the flour.
- Make into a small paste.
- Fry till the golden colour.
- Fry it on high flame.
- Add it in low flame.
- Take them in equal quantity.
- Grate the carrots.
- Shred the beetroot.
- Roast the spices.
- Grind it.
- Take a bowl.
- Mix all the spices together.
- Do not over heat oil.
- Water as needed.
- Mix under low flame.
- Fry till they become crispy.
- Heat two tablespoon of oil.
- Add one teaspoon cumin seeds.

- Add chopped onions.
- Add two dices green chillies.
- Add ginger garlic paste.
- Add half litre of water.
- Add some corn flour.
- Add two spoon of oil.
- Add dhal in hot water.
- Add salt as required.
- Add rice flour little by little.
- Add water little by little and keep stirring without any lumps.
- Add turmeric and stir.
- Boil the dhal for ten minutes
- Cut them in half.
- Add few curry leaves.
- Take two bunches of curry leaves.
- Saute for two minutes.
- Saute under high flame.
- Saute under low flame.
- Saute till raw smell disappears.
- Saute well under medium flame.
- Lower the flame.
- Cook it in medium flame.
- Simmer the flame.
- Cook it for high flame.
- Cook till tomatoes get smooth.
- Cook for 5 more minutes.
- Let it cook for 10 minutes.
- Wait till the water starts boiling.

- Stir for half a minute.
- Stir till the sugar dissolves.
- Peel the shells.
- Coat them on both sides.
- Grease the Idli plates with oil.
- Mix it together.
- Roll the dough up.
- Roll it out.
- Pour the butter over it.
- Cut it into slices.
- Boil it for one hour.
- Add salt according to your taste.
- Take out the tomato peels.
- The mutton is half cooked.
- The meat has cooked well.
- Let the water dry.
- Put the chicken in the oil.
- The masala has cooked now.
- Put the chopped onion.
- Mix and whisk.
- Fry the onion.
- Keep it for marinate.
- Marinate for one hour.
- Marinate for about 2 to 3 hours.
- Serve with ketchup.
- Close the lid for two minutes.
- Cover it with a lid.
- Cook till oil separates from them.

- Take them out.
- Cook fifteen minutes in pressure cooker.
- Add chopped onions into it.
- Fry until a crisp light golden brown.
- Rinse the basmati rice.
- Sprinkle the white sugar.
- Sprinkle the lemon juice.
- Let it cool for ten minutes.
- What are you making?
- I have my grandmother's recipe.
- What ingredients do we need?

22. SAY 'SORRY'

- I am sorry.
- Sorry for the trouble.
- Sorry, I am late.
- Sorry for the delay.
- Sorry, I forgot.
- I am sorry, I cannot go.
- I am sorry, I have to go now.
- Sorry, you can't stay here.
- I am very sorry for what I did.

23. ASKING HELP

- Do you need help?
- Please help me.
- Can you help me, please?

- Would you help me, please?
- Give me a hand, please.

24. OCCUPATION

- What do you do?
- Where do you work?
- Where are you working?
- What is your occupation?
- What is your designation?
- How long have you been working here?
- What is your job there?
- How do you go to office?
- How much money do you earn for a month?
- How much is the salary?
- How long have you been working here?
- I work for myself.
- Do you have any vacancy?
- I am looking for a job.
- I am not working at the moment.
- My father is an Accountant.
- My mother is a Home maker.
- I have my own business.
- Do you have a part-time job?
- I work as a part timer.
- I am doing business.
- I am doing export business.
- He works in an office.
- I am looking for a job.

- He is working as a Teacher in St. John High School.
- He is an Engineer.
- I am a graduate.
- I am a teacher in a private school.
- He is working here for five years.

25. WEATHER

- What is the weather like today?
- Today, the weather is hot.
- The weather is very bad.
- It is sweltering.
- It is cold.
- It is hot and humid.
- It is snowy.
- It is warm.
- It is scorching.
- It is sultry.
- It is overcast.
- It is dark and cloudy.
- It is stormy.
- It is rainy.
- It is cloudy.
- It is windy.
- It is drizzling.
- It is raining.
- It is raining heavily outside.
- It is about to rain.
- It is raining heavily now.

- It has been raining for two hours.
- Did you drench in the rain?
- I got drenched in the rain.
- It kept drizzling all through the night.
- It is drizzling. Take an umbrella.

26. SHOPPING

- May I help you?
- What do you want sir?
- I need a shirt.
- I am just looking.
- I am looking for a formal shirt.
- It is on the first floor.
- It is too loose/long.
- It is too big/small.
- It is too tight.
- Can I try this on?
- Is it wrinkle-free?
- Where can I find shirt?
- Do you have jeans pant?
- Is this on sale?
- Where is men's wear?
- Where is the children's section?
- Let me try it on and see how it fits.
- Please, try this shirt.
- Do you have this in red?
- Do you have a smaller/bigger size?
- Do you have it in larger?

- What size do you want?
- Look at yourself in the mirror.
- I bought this in retail store.
- Is this free?
- I like this one.
- Do you have it in another colour?
- Try this shoe.
- Kids section is in the third floor.
- Excuse me, where is the trial room?
- Where is the changing room?
- Do you have any new model?
- How much is this?
- Is there any discount?
- Can you gift wrap that?
- Where is the billing counter?
- Is there any discount on this?
- It costs too much.
- It is costly.
- It is 20% off.
- I am a regular customer here. Please offer me a better price.
- Can you lower the price?
- The cost is too much.
- It is too expensive.
- The price is cheaper.
- Thank you for shopping with us!
- Could you bring me the bill, please?
- Do you accept credit card?
- Here 500 rupees. You can keep the change.

- The shop opens till 10 o'clock.

27. RESTAURANT

Waiter / Waitress

- May I help you?
- Here's the menu.
- Are you ready to order?
- Any side dish, Sir?
- Would you like anything to drink?
- Would you like coffee or tea?
- Do you want anything?
- Would you like anything else?
- Today's special is garlic fish.
- I am sorry, we are out of fish.
- Let me repeat your order.
- Enjoy your meal.
- What kind of ice cream do you want?
- We have chocolate, vanilla and strawberry.
- Would you like to pay together or separate?
- The total for your lunch is 1500 rupees.
- Thank you, please come again.

Customer

- Excuse me, waiter.
- There are four of us.
- The menu, please.
- Could you bring me the menu, please?

- What is today's special?
- We are ready to order.
- Waiter! Three Dosas.
- Bring two plates of Biriyani.
- I would like to have a Mutton Dosa.
- We would like to order three Veg-Biriyani.
- I want Veg-Biriyani and ice-cream, please.
- Do you have Barbeque Chicken?
- Is there anything to eat?
- What do you recommend? (to waiter)
- Please make this soup 1 by 2.
- May I have a spoon?
- May I have some water, please?
- Can I change my order please?
- What kind of ice cream do you have?
- I want a lemon juice.
- A cup of coffee please.
- We would like 2 coffees and 2 teas.
- Would you bring me some coffee?
- That's all, thank you.

Describing taste

- It is delicious.
- It is sweet.
- It is tasty.
- It is yummy.
- It is sour.
- It is bitter.

- It is spicy.
- It was salty.
- It was awful.
- It was tasteless.
- It was mushy.
- It is stale.
- It is oily.
- It is hot.
- It is crunchy.
- It is rotten.

28. MOVIE / THEATRE

- I saw a movie.
- What time does the movie begin?
- Have you seen this movie?
- We are going to watch a movie.
- Let's go to the movie.
- I have seen that movie.
- I don't like animated movies.
- Who is the director?
- Who directed this movie?
- Do you like movies?
- I like movies a lot.
- Did you like that movie?
- Who is your favorite director?
- Who directed this film?
- Who is the producer?
- Who is the hero?

- The film has already begun.
- Where can I buy tickets?
- How much is the ticket?
- I booked the ticket in online.
- One ticket, please.
- We have already seen this film.
- This film is terrible.
- It is a dubbed movie.
- Did you enjoy the movie?
- Cinematography was excellent.
- The movie will start at 10 am.
- The movie is not that scary.
- I hate action movies.
- Is it a remake?
- He acted as a cameo.
- He is the veteran actor.
- It is a box-office.
- The movie was the biggest flop.
- Have you watched the movie 'The Lion King'?
- How was the movie?
- What kind of film is it?
- It is a romance comedy.
- It was an animated film.
- It was a documentary film.
- It is a slapstick comedy.
- It is an epic movie.
- It is a horror.
- It is a thriller movie.

- It is a 3D movie.
- It was heartwarming. (emotional)
- It was a hilarious. (very funny)
- It is a bang bang film.
- The film was fun.
- The film is superb.
- The film was not good.

29. AT HOSPITAL

- Shall I call a doctor?
- What is the problem?
- Do you have any allergies?
- Do you have a cough?
- What ails you?
- I am not well.
- I feel sick.
- I am bleeding.
- I have asthma.
- I feel feverish.
- I hurt my arm.
- I have a runny nose.
- My stomach hurts.
- I cannot bend over.
- My stomach is upset.
- My legs feel weak.
- My joints are aching.
- I feel lousy.
- I feel cold.

- I have sore gum.
- I banged my head.
- I have sprained my ankle.
- I have a fever.
- I am unwell.
- I feel sick.
- I have cough.
- My arms hurt.
- My face is swollen.
- My eyes are itchy.
- My arm is sore.
- I have got diarrhea.
- I have a headache.
- Are you hurt badly?
- I feel achy.
- My nose is running.
- You are bleeding.
- I am so dizzy I cannot stand.
- I feel dizzy, I don't see well.
- I have got a pain in my chest.
- My skin is itchy, I cannot stop scratching.
- My chest feels tight I can't breathe.
- My throat is dry! I cannot stop coughing.
- I twisted my ankle.
- I have a cold for one week.
- I have got a bruise on my leg.
- I have got a rash on my arm.
- My stomach is gripping.

- I have a sore throat.
- I cannot stop bleeding.
- I am allergic to dust.
- Your rib is broken.
- My ears are sore! I can't hear.
- I have a toothache I think I have a cavity.
- I hurt my leg when I run.
- I am having trouble breathing.
- I have a pain in my left shoulder.
- I have got a cut on my finger.
- My back has been hurting.
- I have a headache.
- I have got a sprained ankle.
- I have a pain in my back.
- Your bone has broken.
- I have a temperature, sore throat.
- I am allergic to antibiotics.
- How long have you feeling like this?
- Do you have any other symptoms?
- Let's check your temperature.
- I sprained my wrist.
- I am going to take your blood pressure.
- What did the doctor say?
- Anything serious doctor?
- Did you sleep well?
- Do you feel better now?
- May I take rice, Doctor?
- How long do you have fever?

- I am going to put an injection.
- Where is the emergency ward?
- Patient is very serious.
- Your blood pressure is normal.
- I will prescribe you some tablets.
- We need to take a urine sample.
- You need to have a blood test.
- I will dress the wound.
- My wound is getting better now.
- I will put the plaster.
- You have a fever.
- My wound is getting better now.
- Don't worry there is no serious problem.
- Take this medicine three times a day, after meal.
- I hope you will get better soon.
- She is carrying a baby.
- When is your due?
- Do you know if it is a boy or a girl?
- She is pregnant.
- Vimala has given birth to a baby girl.

30. ASKING & GIVING DIRECTION

ASKING DIRECTION

- Excuse me, Do you know where the Taj Hotel is?
- Excuse me, Is there a hotel near here?
- Excuse me, Where is the Town Hall road?
- How far is it from here?

- How long does it take to walk there?
- Where is the nearest supermarket?
- Would you show me the way to the Meenakshi Amman temple?

GIVING DIRECTION

- Go straight.
- Take left.
- Take right.
- Turn left.
- Please, Turn right.
- Turn around.
- It is on the left side.
- Go through the market.
- Walk past the Church.
- Walk a little distance.
- Walk along the main road.
- It is in the middle of the block.
- It is not too far.
- It is in the corner.
- It is just around the corner.
- It is about 100 meters.
- It is in the next street.
- It is just opposite to the Temple.
- It is at the end of this street.
- It is in the next building.
- It is just behind that Temple.
- It is very near.
- It is across the street.

- It is opposite to the post office.
- Follow me. I will show you the way.
- I am sorry, I am new here.

31. LIKE & DISLIKE

- I like you.
- I am fond of Ice cream.
- I like it very much.
- She likes you.
- I like Noodles.
- I like your shirt.
- I am crazy about Ajit.
- I do not like it.
- I don't like this film.
- She doesn't like the movie.
- They don't like Anand.
- I do not like him.
- I don't like Biriyani.
- Don't you like me?
- I am not crazy about it.

32. DON'T KNOW

- Sorry, I do not know.
- I have no idea.
- I am not sure about that.
- I don't know anything about it.
- I don't have any information about that.

- I don't know where to go.
- I don't know when will the film start.
- I don't know what they want.
- I don't know what film is it.
- I don't know what happened.
- You don't know how I feel.

33. BUS – TRAIN – TAXI

- Where is the ticket counter?
- Where is the bus stop?
- Where can I buy ticket?
- What time is the next bus to Kerala?
- How much is a single ticket to Chennai?
- I would like a single ticket to Bangalore.
- How much is a first class ticket to Chennai?
- Which bus should I take?
- Has Chennai bus gone?
- The bus will be here soon.
- Here comes the bus.
- I take this bus every day.
- You can buy your ticket at the station.
- How much is the ticket?
- How can I get there?
- Is this the way to ……?
- Is it possible to change the ticket?
- How often does this bus run?
- I reached the railway station.
- I missed the bus.

- I missed my stop.
- It takes 30 minutes to go to the station.
- The train arrived to the station at 10 PM.
- The train has not arrived yet.
- Is there a bus stop near here?
- Does this bus go to University?
- Does the bus stop at the railway station?
- How much is a bus ticket?
- Could you tell me which platform I should go to?
- It is always crowd in the bus.
- I have to stand all the way.
- I am on the train.
- The ticket counter is very crowd.
- I can't get the ticket.
- I booked the ticket in online.
- Where can I find a taxi stand?
- Please call a taxi.
- You should go there by taxi.
- Shall I take a taxi?
- I left my purse in the taxi.
- Do you know where the taxi stand is?
- Is that taxi occupied?
- Is it far from here?
- How long does it take to get there?
- How far is it from hotel to the airport?
- How far is it from here?
- I don't know where to go.
- I need to go to this address.

- I don't know how to get there.
- Take me to this address, please.
- Take me there, please.
- Could you drive a bit faster?
- How many hours it will take?
- How many kilometers are there?
- It will take half an hour, Sir.
- Ok, let's go.
- Could you stop here, please?
- Driver turn left.
- Step on it!
- Hit the break.
- Make a U-turn.
- Turn right here.
- Please stop here.
- Right here, please.
- Get off the bus.
- Get out of the taxi.
- How much should I pay?
- It's Rs200/-.

34. ACCIDENT – DEATH

- Is he alive?
- Is he dead?
- He was crushed to death.
- He passed away in a private hospital.
- He died on the way to hospital.
- He died several years ago.

- He was declared dead.
- He died of fever.
- He is deceased.
- He passed away.
- He is no more.
- He met with an accident.
- It was an accident.
- He lost his wife in a traffic accident.
- He died on the spot.
- He died in a car accident.
- He died of lung cancer.
- He died in a drunk-driving accident.
- He was killed in a road accident.
- Vanitha was hurt in an accident.
- When did the accident happen?
- How did the accident happen?
- Four women were knocked down by a minivan.
- Ten pilgrims were injured in the road accident.
- He was injured in an accident.
- Anand was injured in a traffic accident.
- Luckily, nobody was hurt in the collision.
- Nobody was hurt in the accident.
- Bus rammed into five cars.
- A speeding van rammed it from behind.
- I was shocked to hear about the death of your father.
- I feel sorry for your loss.

35. WAY TO WISH

- Have a splendid New Year.
- Have a New Year filled with prosperity.
- New Year greetings to you and your family.
- Wishing you all the best.
- Best of luck to you.
- Wishing you all success.
- Congratulations to a lovely couple.
- Warm wishes to the newborn baby and parents too.
- All the best to your little baby.
- I wish you a wonderful birthday.
- May your birthday be filled with laughter.
- Many more happy returns of the day.

36. ASKING TO DRINK OR EAT

- Would you like some snacks?
- May I offer you something to drink?
- May I bring you coffee?
- Can I get you some juice?
- Can I offer you something to eat?
- Would you like something to drink?
- Do you need anything?

37. WARNING

- Mind your words.
- Mind your own business.
- Be in your limit.

- Watch your mouth.
- Think before you speak.
- You are messing with a wrong person.
- Keep check on your tongue.
- Don't you dare involve my family.
- How dare you talk to me like this.
- How could you do this to me!
- How dare you!
- I will break your teeth.
- I am warning you.
- Thanks for warning me.
- Don't tease me.
- Don't annoy me.
- Don't try my patience.
- Don't argue with me.
- Who do you think you are!
- None of your business!

38. PHONE

- Hi, this is Rohan.
- Who is this?
- Is this Mr. Arjun?
- Who is it?
- Hello, Is Kamal there?
- Hello, this is Shobana. Who is that?
- Hold the line, please.
- Who is speaking?
- May I speak to Vimal?

- It's me. Who is calling?
- One moment, please.
- Sorry wrong number.
- Please check the number.
- Could I speak to Varsha, please?
- Thank you for calling.
- I will call you later.
- His phone is switched off.
- My battery is dead.
- My battery is low.
- Your phone is still charging.
- I don't have a charger.
- My battery is down.
- Signal is weak.
- I don't have signal.
- It is not reachable.
- Sorry, I had my phone on mute.
- Give me a call when you reach home.
- Send me a message.
- My phone doesn't work.
- May I use your mobile, please?
- Give me a missed call.
- Call me in an hour.
- Don't call me, I will call you.
- If it rings, answer it.
- The phone is ringing.
- Pick up the phone.
- Make a phone call.

- Did you call me?
- Could you say that again, please?
- I am sorry, what did you say?

39. PHONE CHATTING SENTENCES

- When will you be free?
- I like your profile photo.
- Why did you remove your DP?
- Change your DP, It is not a good one.
- I cannot see your DP.
- The photos have been sent to you.
- Let me know when you receive the photo.
- Upload it on your status.
- Why did you upload such status?
- You are off line these days.
- I see you online all the time.
- When will you come online?
- Shall we talk in a video call?
- No, not this time.
- Alright, when is a good time for you?
- When will you come online again?
- I need today's photo.
- Whose number is this?
- She texted me yesterday.
- I couldn't reply on time.
- Why are you replying me late?
- Are you talking to someone else?
- I think you don't want to talk.

- Is anybody around you?
- Have bothered you?
- Talk to me after having food
- Alright, I will talk to you later.
- If you are busy, we can talk later.
- Talk to me properly.
- Do you have bad network?
- Don't make me fool.
- I texted you but you didn't reply.
- I am going to call you.
- I was about to text you.
- You should have sent a voice note.
- Where have you been?
- Where were we?
- Convey my message to him.
- I cannot send today.
- Network is very bad
- Can I send voice message?
- I don't have whatsapp.
- I don't use Social Media.
- Which phone do you use?
- I watch YouTube Channels
- My phone is not updated
- Which phone do you have?
- I need a new phone
- I want to buy a new phone
- Can I talk for a while?
- Send your location

- I am sending you the link
- Click the link and join the group
- Share this link with others.
- Stay within your limit
- It’s none of your business
- I won’t chat with anybody
- I am not addicted to chatting
- I won’t play games in the phone
- I don’t waste my time in Social Media
- If you disturb me, I will complain to the cyber crime.

40. Read and Practice

1. Arun loves his mom and she always takes care of him.
   She cooks tasty dishes for him.
   He loves to sit and eat with her.
   His mother helps him to write his homework.
   Arun also helps his mother to clean the house.
   On Sundays, they go out to many places.
   They have fun together.

2. I am Sophia.
   I am eleven years old.
   I come from Bangalore.
   I am studying seventh standard in Ryan International School.
   My favourite subject is English.
   My hobby is reading storybooks.
   My aim is to become an Author.

3. My teacher's name is Scarlett.
   She teaches us English.
   She also teaches us good habits and moral values.
   She is very intelligent.
   She is kind to everyone.
   She is always punctual.
   She has a good personality.
   All the students like her very much.

4. My hobby is reading books.
   There is no better companion than a good book.
   It makes me to develop my language skills and vocabulary.
   Reading is a good way to relax and reduce stress.

It also improves memory power.
I usually go to the public library in my town and buy many books.

5. My father's name is Jack.
He is 40 years old. He is a Businessman.
He is very kind and hard working.
He loves reading and travelling.
He teaches me good manners and values.
He takes care of the entire family.
I love him very much.

6. My mother's name is Shreya.
She is 34 years old. My mother is a homemaker.
She is a hardworking woman.
She gets up early in the morning.
Every day she cooks delicious food for us.
She takes care of everyone in the house.
My mother is my first teacher.
She helps me with my homework.
My mother teaches me good things.
I love my mother very much.

7. My name is Sam.
I am 12 years old.
I am studying seventh standard in Ryan Public School.
My father's name is Kevin.
He is fourty. He is an Engineer.
My mother's name is Daisy.

She is 35. She is a homemaker.
I have a sister. Her name is Anitha.
She is eighteen. She is studying in college.

8. I live in a small house in the middle of the city.
I live with my parents and a younger sister.
Our house has two bedrooms, one living room, one bathroom and a kitchen.
We watch TV in the living room.
My sister and I share the same room.
We have a small garden. We have planted many different types of plants and vegetables in the garden.
I do my homework in the bedroom.
Our house is nice and beautiful.

41. Basic Question Answers for Kids

- What is your name?
  My name is Reema.

- How are you?
  I am fine, thank you.

- Where are you from?
  I am from Chennai.

- How old are you?
  I am seven years old.

- What is your father's name?
  My father's name is Rajesh.

- What is your mother's name?
  My mother's name is Priya.

- Where do you live?
  I live in Chennai.

- What is your school name?
  My school name is ABC Public School.

- What class are you in?
  I am in third class.

- Who is your class teacher?
  My class teacher is Mrs. Lakshmi.

- What time do you get up?
  I get up at 6 o'clock.

- What do you do after waking up?
  I brush my teeth.

- What do you have for breakfast?
  I eat idli and dosa.

- When do you go to school?
  I go to school at 8 o'clock.

- How do you go to school?
  I go by bus.

- What do you do at school?
  I study and play.

- What do you eat for lunch?
  I eat curd rice and pickle.

- When do you come home?
  I come home at 4 o'clock.

- What do you do in the evening?
  I play with my friends.

- What time do you sleep?
  I sleep at 9 o'clock.

- How many members are there in your family?
  There are four members.

- Do you have a brother?
  Yes, I have one brother.

- Do you have a sister?
  No, I don't have a sister.

- Who is your best friend?
  My best friend is Anu.

- What do you like to play with your friend?
  I like to play hide and seek.

- What does your father do?
  He is a teacher.

- What does your mother do?
  She is a homemaker.

- Do you love your parents?
  Yes, very much.

- Who helps you in your homework?
  My mother helps me.

- Who cooks food at home?
  My mother cooks food.

- What is your favourite food?
  My favourite food is biryani.

- Do you like fruits?
  Yes, I like fruits.

- Which fruit do you like?
  I like mango.

- What do you drink in the morning?
  I drink milk.

- Do you like ice cream?
  Yes, I love ice cream.

- What is your favourite colour of ice cream?
  Chocolate flavor.

- What do you eat for dinner?
  I eat chapati and curry.

- Do you like vegetables?
  Yes, I do.

- Which vegetable do you like?
  I like potato.

- Do you eat junk food?
  No, I don't eat.

- What subject do you like most?
  I like English.

- Who is your English teacher?
  My English teacher is Mrs. Reema.

- What do you use to write?
  I use a pencil.

- What is your favourite subject?
  My favourite subject is Science.

- Do you like to read books?
  Yes, I do.

- Do you like to play in school?
  Yes, I love to play.

- What is your favourite game?
  My favourite game is cricket.

- Do you like drawing?
  Yes, I like drawing pictures.

- What colour do you use most?
  I use blue colour.

- Do you like your school?
  Yes, very much.

- What do you do at home?
  I play and study.

- Who cleans your room?
  My mother cleans my room.

- Do you help your parents?
  Yes, I help them.

- What do you do on Sundays?
  I watch TV and play games.

- Where do you sleep?
  I sleep in my room.

- What do you do before sleeping?
  I pray and go to bed.

- Do you watch TV?
  Yes, I watch cartoons.

- What is your favourite cartoon?
  My favourite cartoon is Tom and Jerry.

- Do you have toys?
  Yes, I have many toys.

- Which toy do you like most?
  I like my teddy bear.

- Do you like animals?
  Yes, I like animals.

- What is your favourite animal?
  My favourite animal is a dog.

- Do you have a pet?
  Yes, I have a cat.

- What does a dog say?
  A dog says bow-bow.

- What does a cat say?
  A cat says meow-meow.

- What does a cow give us?
  A cow gives us milk.

- Where do birds live?
  Birds live in nests.

- Can a fish fly?
  No, a fish cannot fly.

- Can a bird swim?
  Some birds can swim.

- Which animal is the king of the jungle?
  The lion is the king of the jungle.

- What do you see in the sky?
  I see the sun, moon, and stars.

- What colour is the sky?
  The sky is blue.

- What gives us light?
  The sun gives us light.

- What gives us air?
  Trees give us air.

- What do you see in the garden?
  I see flowers and butterflies.

- What is the color of grass?
  Grass is green.

- Do you like flowers?
  Yes, I like flowers.

- What is your favourite flower?
  My favourite flower is a rose.

- Do trees give us shade?
  Yes, they do.

- What do plants need to grow?
  Plants need water and sunlight.

- How is the weather today?
  It is sunny.

- Do you like rainy days?
  Yes, I like to play in the rain.

- What do you use in the rain?
  I use an umbrella.

- What do you wear in winter?
  I wear a sweater.

- What season do you like most?
  I like summer.

- What do you eat in summer?
  I eat ice cream and fruits.

- What do you drink in summer?
  I drink juice and water.

- What do you see in the rainy season?
  I see clouds and rainbows.

- Do you like cold weather?
  Yes, I like cold weather.

- What do you wear in the rainy season?
  I wear a raincoat.

- What are you wearing?
  I am wearing a blue dress.

- What colour do you like most?
  I like pink colour.

- What do you wear to school?
  I wear my school uniform.

- What do you wear at home?
  I wear casual clothes.

- What do you wear at night?
  I wear nightdress.

- What colour is your bag?
  My bag is red.

- What colour is your shoes?
  My shoes are black.

- Do you wear socks?
  Yes, I wear socks.

- Do you like new clothes?
  Yes, I love new clothes.

- What colour is your hat?
  My hat is yellow.

- What is your favourite festival?
  My favourite festival is Diwali.

- What do you do on Diwali?
  I light lamps and burst crackers.

- Do you like sweets?
  Yes, I love sweets.

- What do you wear on festivals?
  I wear new clothes.

- Do you like Christmas?
  Yes, I like Christmas.

- Who gives gifts on Christmas?
  Santa Claus gives gifts.

- What do you decorate on Christmas?
  I decorate the Christmas tree.

- Do you like Pongal?
  Yes, I like Pongal very much.

- What do people cook on Pongal?
  They cook sweet rice.

- What do you do on your birthday?
  I cut a cake and play with friends.

- What is your hobby?
  My hobby is drawing.

- Do you like reading?
  Yes, I like reading stories.

- Do you like to dance?
  Yes, I love to dance.

- Can you sing?
  Yes, I can sing a song.

- Do you like to paint?
  Yes, I like painting.

- What games do you play?
  I play cricket and carrom.

- Do you like to swim?
  Yes, I like swimming.

- Do you play outdoor games?
  Yes, I do.

- Do you watch cartoons?
  Yes, every day.

- Who is your favourite cartoon character?
  My favourite is Doraemon.

- How do you go to school?
  I go by bus.

- What do you see on the road?
  I see cars and bikes.

- Do you travel by car?
  Yes, sometimes.

- Do you like trains?
  Yes, I like trains.

- Have you seen an airplane?
  Yes, I have seen one.

- What colour is a school bus?
  It is yellow.

- Where does a train run?
  It runs on tracks.

- Who drives a car?
  My driver drives a car.

- Who flies an airplane?
  A pilot flies an airplane.

- Who drives a bus?
  A bus driver drives a bus.

- What time do you wake up?
  I wake up at 6 o'clock.

- What time do you go to bed?
  I go to bed at 9 o'clock.

- How many days are in a week?
  There are seven days.

- What is the first day of the week?
  Sunday is the first day.

- What is the last day of the week?
  Saturday is the last day.

- What day do you like most?
  I like Sunday.

- How many months are in a year?
  There are twelve months.

- Which month is your birthday?
  My birthday is in May.

- Which is the coldest month?
  December is the coldest month.

- Which is the hottest month?
  May is the hottest month.

- Are you happy today?
  Yes, I am happy.

- When do you feel sad?
  When I lose my toy.

- When do you laugh?
  When I watch funny videos.

- What makes you angry?
  When someone breaks my toys.

- When do you feel scared?
  At night in the dark.

- When do you feel excited?
  On my birthday.

- Do you get angry easily?
  No, I don't.

- How do you feel when you get a gift?
  I feel very happy.

- What makes you cry?
  When I get hurt.

- What makes you smile?
  When I play with my friends.

- Can you listen carefully?
  Yes, I can.

- Who tells you stories?
  My grandmother tells me stories.

- Do you listen to music?
  Yes, I like music.

- Do you speak English?
  Yes, a little.

- Do you like to learn new words?
  Yes, I love learning.

- Who teaches you English?
  My English teacher.

- Can you speak loudly?
  Yes, I can.

- Do you like to sing rhymes?
  Yes, I sing rhymes every day.

- Which rhyme do you like most?
  I like "Twinkle, Twinkle, Little Star."

- How many eyes do you have?
  I have two eyes.

- How many ears do you have?
  I have two ears.

- How many hands do you have?
  I have two hands.

- How many legs do you have?
  I have two legs.

- What do you do with your eyes?
  I see with my eyes.

- What do you do with your ears?
  I hear with my ears.

- What do you do with your mouth?
  I eat and talk with my mouth.

- What do you do with your hands?
  I write and play with my hands.

- Do you brush your teeth daily?
  Yes, every morning.

- Do you take a bath daily?
  Yes, I do.

- Do you eat fruits daily?
  Yes, I eat fruits.

- Do you drink water?
  Yes, I drink plenty of water.

- Do you wash your hands before eating?
  Yes, always.

- Do you like junk food?
  Only sometimes.

- What should we drink more?
  We should drink water.

- Do you exercise?
  Yes, in the morning.

- Do you go to the doctor?
  Yes, when I am sick.

- What do you do when you sneeze?
  I cover my mouth.

- Do you sleep well?
  Yes, I sleep well at night.

- Is milk good for health?
  Yes, it is.

- Do you say thank you?
  Yes, I do.

- Do you say sorry?
  Yes, when I make a mistake.

- Do you say please?
  Yes, when I ask something.

- Do you say good morning?
  Yes, every day.

- Do you respect elders?
  Yes, I do.

- Do you share your toys?
  Yes, I share them.

- Do you help your friends?
  Yes, always.

- Do you obey your parents?
  Yes, I do.

- Do you tell lies?
  No, I never lie.

- Do you pray every day?
  Yes, I do.

- What is this?
  This is a book.

- What is that?
  That is a chair.

- Who is he?
  He is my brother.

- Who is she?
  She is my sister.

- Where is your bag?
  My bag is on the table.

- Where is the cat?
  The cat is under the chair.

- What are you doing?
  I am writing.

- What are you eating?
  I am eating rice.

- What are you playing?
  I am playing cricket.

- What are you reading?
  I am reading a storybook.

- Where do you study?
  I study in the classroom.

- Who teaches you English?
  My English teacher teaches me.

- What is on the table?
  A book is on the table.

- What is in your bag?
  Books and pencils are in my bag.

- Do you have a pencil?
  Yes, I have one.

- Do you have an eraser?
  Yes, I do.

- Do you have a pen?
  No, I use a pencil.

- Where is your notebook?
  My notebook is in my bag.

- Do you listen to your teacher?
  Yes, I always listen.

- Do you like to study?
  Yes, I like to study.

- What subject do you like?
  I like Maths.

- Can you count numbers?
  Yes, I can.

- Can you read English?
  Yes, I can read.

- Can you write your name?
  Yes, I can write it.

- Can you spell your name?
  Yes, I can spell it.

- Do you do homework daily?
  Yes, every day.

- Do you read storybooks?
  Yes, I love stories.

- Do you like drawing?
  Yes, I like drawing pictures.

- Who helps you study?
  My parents help me.

- How many rooms are in your house?
  There are five rooms.

- What do you see in the kitchen?
  I see vessels and a stove.

- What do you see in the bedroom?
  I see a bed and pillow.

- What do you see in the living room?
  I see a sofa and TV.

- Where do you eat food?
  I eat in the dining room.

- Where do you keep your toys?
  I keep them in my box.

- Who cleans the house?
  My mother cleans the house.

- Do you have a fan in your room?
  Yes, I have one.

- Do you have a TV?
  Yes, we have a TV.

- Do you help clean your room?
  Yes, I do.

- Who teaches you in school?
  My teacher teaches me.

- Who gives you medicine?
  The doctor gives me medicine.

- Who brings letters?
  The postman brings letters.

- Who catches thieves?
  The policeman catches thieves.

- Who cuts hair?
  The barber cuts hair.

- Who makes shoes?
  The cobbler makes shoes.

- Who builds houses?
  The mason builds houses.

- Who grows crops?
  The farmer grows crops.

- Who repairs cars?
  The mechanic repairs cars.

- Who sells vegetables?
  The vegetable seller sells vegetables.

- What is your favourite fruit?
  Mango is my favourite fruit.

- What colour is a banana?
  It is yellow.

- What colour is an apple?
  It is red.

- What is your favourite vegetable?
  I like potato.

- Do you eat carrots?
  Yes, I do.

- Do you like tomatoes?
  Yes, I like them.

- Do you eat green vegetables?
  Yes, I eat them.

- What do we make from milk?
  We make butter and curd.

- What is your favourite drink?
  My favourite drink is juice.

- Do you like chocolate?
  Yes, I love chocolate.

- Can ants fly?
  No, they can't.

- What is the colour of a crow?
  It is black.

- What is the colour of a parrot?
  It is green.

- What do bees make?
  Bees make honey.

- Where do birds live?
  Birds live in nests.

- Can you name a big bird?
  Yes, an eagle.

- Do you like butterflies?
  Yes, they are beautiful.

- Do you see birds in the morning?
  Yes, they sing in the morning.

- What colour is the sky?
  It is blue.

- What colour is the sun?
  It is yellow.

- What colour is grass?
  It is green.

- What colour is milk?
  It is white.

- What colour are your shoes?
  They are black.

- What colour is your bag?
  It is red.

- What shape is a ball?
  It is round.

- What shape is a clock?
  It is circle.

- What shape is a star?
  It is star-shaped.

- What are you doing?
  I am reading.

- What is she doing?
  She is dancing.

- What is he doing?
  He is eating.

- What are they doing?
  They are playing.

- What is the cat doing?
  The cat is sleeping.

- What is the boy doing?
  The boy is running.

- What is the girl doing?
  The girl is singing.

- What is your mother doing?
  She is cooking.

- What is your father doing?
  He is reading the newspaper.

- What is the baby doing?
  The baby is crying.

- Where do you go to buy books?
  I go to the bookshop.

- Where do you go to study?
  I go to school.

- Where do you go to play?
  I go to the park.

- Where do you go to buy vegetables?
  I go to the market.

- Where do you go to see animals?
  I go to the zoo.

- Where do you go when you are sick?
  I go to the hospital.

- Where do you go to pray?
  I go to the temple.

- Where do you go to buy medicines?
  I go to the pharmacy.

- What do you do in the morning?
  I brush my teeth.

- What do you do after breakfast?
  I get ready for school.

- What do you do at school?
  I study and play.

- What do you do after school?
  I eat snacks.

- What do you do in the evening?
  I play with my friends.

- What do you do at night?
  I read and sleep.

- Do you help your parents?
  Yes, I do.

- Do you water plants?
  Yes, I water plants.

- Do you clean your table?
  Yes, I clean it.

- Do you keep your books properly?
  Yes, always.

- Do you like apples?
  Yes, I do.

- Can you jump?
  Yes, I can.

- Can you drive a car?
  No, I can't.

- Do you play cricket?
  Yes, I play cricket.

- Do you watch TV?
  Yes, every day.

- Can you sing songs?
  Yes, I can sing.

- Can you ride a bicycle?
  Yes, I can ride.

- Do you like to draw?
  Yes, I do.

- Can you swim?
  Yes, a little.

- Have you seen the sea?
  Yes, I have seen it.

- Have you been to a zoo?
  Yes, I have.

- Have you travelled by train?
  Yes, many times.

- Have you seen mountains?
  Yes, they are big.

- Have you been to a park?
  Yes, I go often.

- What do you see in the zoo?
  I see animals.

- What do you see in the park?
  I see trees and swings.

- Do you like holidays?
  Yes, I love holidays.

- Where do you go on holidays?
  I go to my grandparents' house.

- Do you travel by bus?
  Yes, sometimes.

- Do you keep your books neatly?
  Yes, I keep them neat.

- Do you respect teachers?
  Yes, I respect them.

- Do you help old people?
  Yes, I do.

- Do you throw waste on the road?
  No, I don't.

- Do you save water?
  Yes, I save water.

- Do you waste food?
  No, I never waste food.

- Do you share with friends?
  Yes, I share my toys.

- What is the opposite of hot?
  Cold.

- What is the opposite of big?
  Small.

- What is the opposite of day?
  Night.

- What is the opposite of tall?
  Short.

- What colour is your dress?
  It is blue.

- How is the weather today?
  It is sunny.

- How do you feel today?
  I feel happy.

- How is your friend?
  She is fine.

- What is your favourite color?
  My favourite color is pink.

- What is your favourite subject?
  My favourite subject is English.

- What is your favourite animal?
  My favourite animal is a dog.

- Which season do you like most?
  I like winter.

- What do you wear in winter?
  I wear sweaters.

- What do you see in the rainy season?
  I see clouds and rainbows.

- What grows on trees?
  Fruits grow on trees.

- What do you see in the sky at night?
  I see stars and the moon.

- What do you see in the morning sky?
  I see a sun.

- What do you see after rain?
  I see a rainbow.

- What gives us light?
  The sun gives us light.

- What gives us air?
  Trees give us air.

- What gives us rain?
  Clouds give us rain.

- How are you today?
  I am fine, thank you.

- What are you doing now?
  I am reading.

- Do you like mangoes?
  Yes, I do.

- What's your favourite subject?
  My favourite subject is Science.

- Where is your book?
  It is on the table.

- Who is your best friend?
  My best friend is Anitha.

- When do you go to school?
  I go to school at 8 o'clock.

- What do you do on Sundays?
  I play and watch TV.

- Where do you live?
  I live in Chennai.

- What is your school name?
  My school name is Globe.

- What do you say when you meet someone?
  I say "Hello."

- What do you say when you ask for help?
  Please help me.

- What do you say when you meet your teacher?
  Good morning, teacher.

- What do you say when you come home?
  I'm home, Mom!

- Are you happy?
  Yes, I am happy.

- Are you a student?
  Yes, I am.

- Is he your friend?
  Yes, he is.

- Is she your sister?
  Yes, she is.

- Are they your parents?
  Yes, they are.

- Is it raining?
  Yes, it is.

- Is the dog sleeping?
  Yes, it is sleeping.

- Are you ready?
  Yes, I am ready.

- Are you tired?
  No, I'm not.

- Are you feeling good?
  Yes, I am feeling good.

- Do you help your friends?
  Yes, always.

- Do you share your snacks?
  Yes, I do.

- Do you love your parents?
  Yes, very much.

- Do you take care of your pets?
  Yes, I do.

- Do you help your mother?
  Yes, I help her.

- Do you visit your grandparents?
  Yes, I visit them.

- Do you greet your neighbors?
  Yes, I greet them.

- Do you help others in need?
  Yes, I try to help.

- Do you smile often?
  Yes, I smile every day.

- Who are you?
  I am a student.

- Where do you live?
  I live in India.

- What do you like?
  I like music.

- What do you want to be?
  I want to be a teacher.

- Who is calling you?
  My friend is calling me.

- What are you writing?
  I am writing a story.

- What is your favourite toy?
  My favourite toy is a car.

- What do you like to draw?
  I like to draw flowers.

- What is your favourite rhyme?
  My favourite rhyme is “Johnny Johnny.”

- What game do you play at school?
  I play football.

- What colour is your lunch box?
  It is red.

- Do you like to dance?
  Yes, I love dancing.

- Who packs your lunch?
  My mother packs my lunch.

- Who wakes you up in the morning?
  My mom wakes me up.

- What do you drink in the morning?
  I drink milk.

- What do you wear to school?
  I wear my uniform.

- What do you see in the garden?
  I see flowers and butterflies.

- What do you see in the sky?
  I see clouds and the sun.

- What do you see in the market?
  I see shops and people.

- What do you see on the road?
  I see cars and buses.

- What do you see in the classroom?
  I see my teacher and friends.

- What do you see in the kitchen?
  I see plates and spoons.

- What do you see in the bathroom?
  I see soap and towel.

- What do you see in the park?
  I see trees and swings.

- What do you see in the zoo?
  I see animals.

- What do you see in the playground?
  I see children playing.

- Why do we eat food?
  I eat food to get energy.

- Why do we sleep?
  To get rest.

- Why do we go to school?
  We go to school to learn.

- Why do we brush our teeth?
  To keep them clean.

- Why do we wear clothes?
  To cover our body.

- Why do we drink water?
  To stay healthy.

- Why do we exercise?
  To stay fit.

- Why do we study?
  To gain knowledge.

- Why do we help others?
  Because it is good to help others.

- What time do you eat breakfast?
  At 8 o'clock.

- What time do you sleep?
  I sleep at 9:30 p.m.

- What time do you go to school?
  I go to school at 8 o'clock.

- What time do you come home?
  At 4 o'clock.

- What do you do on your birthday?
  I cut a cake.

- What do you do in summer?
  I eat ice cream.

- What do you do in winter?
  I wear warm clothes.

- What do you do when it rains?
  I use an umbrella.

- What do you do when you feel tired?
  I take rest.

- What do you do when you are happy?
  I smile and laugh.

- Who is your hero?
  My father is my hero.

- What do you love most?
  I love my family.

- Who is your favourite teacher?
  My English teacher.

- What is your favourite song?
  Twinkle Twinkle Little Star.

- Do you like stories?
  Yes, I love them.

- Do you like school?
  Yes, I like it very much.

- What is your favourite book?
  My favourite book is my storybook.

- Who tells you bedtime stories?
  My grandmother.

- Who is your best friend?
  My best friend is Kavin.

- Do you like your friends?
  Yes, I love them.

- Are you a good child?
  Yes, I am.

- Do you listen to your parents?
  Yes, I always listen.

- Do you speak truth?
  Yes, I do.

- Do you smile every day?
  Yes, I smile daily.

- Do you love animals?
  Yes, I love them.

- Do you like reading books?
  Yes, I do.

- Are you kind to others?
  Yes, I am kind.

- Are you helpful?
  Yes, I help everyone.

- Are you honest?
  Yes, I am honest.

- Are you hardworking?
  Yes, I am hardworking.

- Do you love your country?
  Yes, I love my country.

- What do you want to become?
  I want to become a doctor.

- What will you do when you grow up?
  I will help people.

- Do you like your school?
  Yes, I love it.

- Do you like English?
  Yes, it's fun!

- Do you like learning new words?
  Yes, I do.

- Do you like speaking English?
  Yes, very much!

Subject	Verb Present	Verb Past
I	am	was
He	is	was
She	is	was
It	is	was
We	are	were
You	are	were
They	are	were
He	has	had
She	has	had
It	has	had
I	have	had
We	have	had
You	have	had
They	have	had
I	do	did
We	do	did
You	do	did
They	do	did
He	does	did
She	does	did
It	does	did